GHENT TRAVEL GUIDE 2025

GUIDE 2025

Discover the Hidden Gems, Iconic Attractions, and Local Experiences

CLIFFORD WINFRED

TABLE OF CONTENT

Credit@google

INTRODUCTION

Credit@google

Welcome to Ghent, a vibrant city that beautifully marries history and modernity. With its picturesque canals, medieval architecture, and a thriving cultural scene, Ghent is a hidden gem in Belgium that invites exploration. Whether you're wandering through cobblestone streets, indulging in delicious local cuisine, or immersing yourself in the rich history of its landmarks, Ghent offers a unique experience that caters to every traveler.

How to Use This Guide

Navigating a new city can be overwhelming, especially one as rich in history and culture as Ghent. This guide is designed to serve as your trusted companion, providing you with the information and tools necessary to explore Ghent confidently and enjoyably. Here's how to make the most of this guide:

1. *Understand the Structure*

This guide is organized into clear chapters, each focusing on different aspects of Ghent. You'll find information grouped logically, making it easy to find what you need. Here's a brief overview of how the chapters are structured:

- Overview of the City: Get acquainted with Ghent's historical significance, unique features, and compelling reasons to visit.
- Planning Your Trip: Essential tips for scheduling your visit, including best times to go and travel essentials.

- Getting to Ghent: Detailed information on transportation options to reach Ghent, whether by air, train, or car.

- Accommodation: Recommendations for various types of lodging, catering to all budgets.

- Exploring the Attractions: Highlights of must-see sights, including operation hours, entry fees, and interesting facts.

- Dining and Culinary Scene: A guide to local delicacies, restaurants, and food experiences.

- Shopping: Insight into shopping districts, local markets, and what to buy.

- Nightlife and Entertainment: An overview of Ghent's vibrant nightlife and cultural scene.

- Day Trips and Nearby Destinations: Suggestions for excursions beyond the city limits.

- Practical Tips: Local customs, language basics, currency information, and safety tips.

- Itinerary Ideas: Sample itineraries tailored for different interests and travel styles.

- Getting Around: Transportation options within Ghent, including public transport and bike rentals.

- Local Events and Festivals: Information on annual events that enhance the Ghent experience.

- Sustainability and Responsible Tourism: Tips for being a responsible traveler and supporting local communities.

2. *Use the Index and Glossary*

At the end of this guide, you'll find a comprehensive index and glossary. The index allows you to quickly locate specific topics or attractions, while the glossary provides definitions for local terms, phrases, and key concepts. This feature is particularly useful if you encounter unfamiliar terms related to Ghent's culture or history.

3. *Consult the Maps*

Throughout the guide, you will find maps highlighting key areas of interest. These maps are designed to give you a visual understanding of Ghent's layout, helping you plan your route efficiently. Pay close attention to the marked attractions, accommodations, and dining options to streamline your explorations.

4. *Plan Your Itinerary*

Each chapter includes tips and suggestions to help you plan your itinerary. Whether you have a day or a week to spend in Ghent, you can customize your visit based on your interests. The itinerary ideas in Chapter 11 provide structured plans, while the practical tips and attractions sections allow you to mix and match experiences according to your preferences.

5. *Take Advantage of Local Insights*

This guide is enriched with local insights and personal recommendations. As you read through each section, look for highlighted tips and insider knowledge that can enhance your experience. From the best times to visit certain attractions to hidden gems known only to locals, these insights will help you discover the authentic side of Ghent.

6. *Stay Updated*

While this guide provides valuable information, it's essential to stay updated on any changes that may occur, such as opening hours, entry fees, and local events. Websites, social media, and local tourism offices are excellent resources for the latest information. Consider downloading apps related to public transport or attractions for real-time updates during your visit.

7. *Engage with the Community*

Ghent is known for its friendly locals and vibrant culture. Don't hesitate to engage with residents, whether through casual conversations or by participating in local events. The insights you gain from interactions with locals can enrich your experience, providing a deeper understanding of Ghent's traditions and lifestyle.

8. *Practice Responsible Tourism*

As you explore Ghent, keep in mind the principles of responsible tourism. Respect local customs and the environment, and support local businesses whenever possible. This guide includes a chapter on sustainability and responsible tourism, providing you with ideas on how to minimize your impact while enjoying your trip.

9. *Document Your Journey*

Consider keeping a travel journal or blog during your time in Ghent. Documenting your experiences not only helps you remember the moments you've cherished but also provides an opportunity to reflect on your journey. Additionally, sharing your experiences can inspire others to explore Ghent and discover its beauty.

10. *Enjoy the Journey*

Lastly, remember that travel is about enjoying the journey. While this guide provides a roadmap for your trip, don't hesitate to venture off the beaten path. Allow for spontaneity in your itinerary, as some of the best experiences often come from unexpected discoveries.

About the Author: A Love Affair with Ghent

As a passionate traveler and admirer of Ghent, I have spent countless hours exploring its hidden corners, engaging with its locals, and indulging in its culinary delights. This guide reflects my love affair with the city, aiming to share the magic of Ghent with you. I hope my insights and recommendations inspire you to discover all that this enchanting city has to offer.

CHAPTER 1: OVERVIEW OF THE CITY

Credit@google

Welcome to Ghent

Nestled at the confluence of the Rivers Lys and Scheldt, Ghent is one of Belgium's most captivating cities, blending a rich historical heritage with a lively contemporary culture. As the capital of the East Flanders province, Ghent offers a unique mix of medieval charm and modern sophistication, making it an ideal destination for travelers seeking both history and vibrancy.

Walking through Ghent's cobblestone streets, visitors are greeted by an enchanting atmosphere, characterized by picturesque canals, stunning architecture, and a vibrant arts scene. The city's historical buildings, including the iconic Gravensteen Castle and the majestic Saint Bavo's Cathedral, narrate stories of its glorious past, while a plethora of trendy cafes, boutiques, and cultural venues illustrate its dynamic present. Whether you're here for a weekend getaway or a longer stay, Ghent promises an unforgettable experience steeped in culture, culinary delights, and captivating sights.

Brief History

Ghent's history dates back to Roman times, when it was known as "Ganda," a settlement that thrived due to its strategic location along trade routes. However, it wasn't until the Middle Ages that Ghent emerged as a significant urban center. By the 12th century, it had developed into one of the largest and wealthiest cities in Europe, primarily due to its booming textile industry. The city became a hub for trade and commerce, attracting merchants from across the continent.

The 14th century marked a golden age for Ghent, with the construction of impressive structures like the Saint Bavo's Cathedral and the expansion of the city's fortifications. During this time, Ghent became a leading center of the Flemish revolt against the oppressive rule of the Burgundian dukes, showcasing the city's resilience and spirit of independence.

In the following centuries, Ghent experienced various political changes, including occupation by foreign powers and industrialization in the 19th century, which further transformed its landscape.

The city's rich history is reflected in its architecture, museums, and vibrant cultural traditions, which continue to thrive today.

Why Visit Ghent

Ghent is often overshadowed by its more famous neighbors, such as Bruges and Antwerp, but this city has much to offer, making it a worthwhile destination in its own right. Here are several compelling reasons to include Ghent on your travel itinerary:

1. **Historical Charm**: Ghent's medieval architecture, including the well-preserved buildings

and charming canals, provides a glimpse into the past. Visitors can explore the iconic Gravensteen Castle, stroll along the historic Graslei and Korenlei streets, and admire the stunning Gothic facades.

2. *Cultural Richness*: The city is home to numerous museums and galleries, showcasing everything from contemporary art to ancient artifacts. The Museum of Fine Arts and the STAM City Museum offer fascinating insights into Ghent's artistic heritage.

3. *Culinary Delights*: Ghent boasts a thriving culinary scene, with a plethora of restaurants, cafes, and local markets where visitors can savor traditional Flemish dishes and innovative cuisine.

Don't miss the chance to try local specialties such as waterzooi and stoverij.

4. *Vibrant Festivals*: Ghent hosts a variety of festivals throughout the year, celebrating everything from music and arts to gastronomy and culture. The Gentse Feesten, held every July, is one of the largest cultural festivals in Belgium, featuring performances, parades, and street food.

5. *Sustainable Initiatives*: Ghent is recognized for its commitment to sustainability and eco-friendly practices. The city encourages cycling and walking, making it easy for visitors to explore its attractions while minimizing their environmental impact.

6. *Accessibility*: Located at the crossroads of major Belgian cities, Ghent is easily accessible by train, making it a convenient base for exploring the broader region.

Key Facts and Figures

- *Population*: Approximately 260,000 residents make Ghent a lively yet manageable city to explore.
- *Area*: Ghent covers an area of about 156.18 square kilometers (60.4 square miles), offering a diverse landscape of urban and green spaces.

- *Language*: The primary language spoken in Ghent is Dutch, although many residents also speak French and English, especially in tourist areas.

- *Currency*: Belgium uses the Euro (€). Credit and debit cards are widely accepted, but it's always advisable to have some cash on hand for small purchases.

- *Climate*: Ghent experiences a temperate maritime climate, with mild summers and cool winters. Average temperatures range from 1°C (34°F) in January to 23°C (73°F) in July. Rain is common throughout the year, so packing an umbrella is advisable.

summary

Ghent is a city that beckons to be explored, offering a rich tapestry of history, culture, and modern-day vibrancy. From its historical landmarks and artistic endeavors to its culinary delights and commitment to sustainability, Ghent promises an enriching experience for every traveler. As you delve into the chapters of this guide, you will discover the many facets of this remarkable city, helping you to plan a memorable visit.

CHAPTER 2: PLANNING YOUR TRIP

Credit@google

Best Time to Visit

Choosing the right time to visit Ghent can significantly enhance your travel experience. Each season offers unique attractions and activities, allowing you to tailor your visit according to your preferences.

- **Spring (March to May):** Spring is a delightful time to visit Ghent, as the city comes alive with blooming flowers and mild temperatures. The pleasant weather makes it ideal for exploring outdoor attractions and enjoying the vibrant atmosphere of local parks. Events such as the Ghent Floralies, a major flower and plant exhibition, take place in April, showcasing stunning floral arrangements and designs.

- **Summer (June to August):** Summer is peak tourist season in Ghent. The long days and warm weather are perfect for outdoor activities, festivals, and enjoying the city's bustling terraces. The Gentse Feesten, a large cultural festival, occurs in July, featuring music, street performances, and culinary delights. However, be prepared for larger crowds and higher accommodation prices during this time.

- *Autumn (September to November):* Autumn is another excellent time to visit, with mild temperatures and fewer tourists. The fall foliage adds a beautiful touch to the city's landscapes. September marks the start of the local harvest season, offering opportunities to taste seasonal dishes in restaurants. Additionally, the city hosts various art and cultural events, making it a vibrant time to experience Ghent.

- *Winter (December to February):* Winters in Ghent can be chilly, with temperatures often dropping below freezing. However, the city transforms into a winter wonderland during this season. The Christmas market, held in December, offers a festive atmosphere with holiday lights, local crafts, and delicious seasonal treats. If you don't mind the cold, winter is a magical time to explore the city's cozy cafes and historical sites.

Duration of Stay

The ideal duration for your stay in Ghent largely depends on your interests and the depth of exploration you desire. However, a well-planned visit can be enjoyed in the following timeframes:

- **Weekend Getaway (2-3 Days):** A short visit allows you to experience the highlights of Ghent, including major attractions like Gravensteen Castle, Saint Bavo's Cathedral, and the picturesque Graslei and Korenlei streets. You can also enjoy a taste of the local cuisine and explore a few museums.

- **Extended Stay (4-5 Days):** With a few extra days, you can delve deeper into Ghent's cultural offerings, visit more museums, and participate in local events or festivals. This duration allows you to take leisurely strolls along the canals, sample local delicacies, and even take day trips to nearby cities like Bruges or Antwerp.

- *Week or More:* For those wanting a more immersive experience, spending a week or more in Ghent opens up opportunities for exploring the surrounding countryside, enjoying leisurely meals at local restaurants, and engaging with the local community. You can also consider joining guided tours or workshops that showcase local arts, crafts, and culinary traditions.

Travel Essentials

To ensure a smooth and enjoyable trip to Ghent, it's essential to prepare adequately. Here are some travel essentials to consider:

- *Travel Insurance:* While it's not mandatory, travel insurance is highly recommended to cover any unforeseen events, such as trip cancellations, medical emergencies, or lost luggage.

- *Currency*: Belgium uses the Euro (€). Make sure to carry some cash for small purchases, although credit and debit cards are widely accepted. ATMs are readily available throughout the city.

- *Local SIM Card or Roaming Plan:* If you need internet access during your trip, consider purchasing a local SIM card or checking with your provider about international roaming plans. Wi-Fi is also available in many cafes and public spaces.

- *Power Adapters*: Belgium uses the standard European plug type (C and E) with a voltage of 230V. Ensure you have the appropriate power adapters for your electronic devices.

- *Comfortable Footwear:* Ghent is best explored on foot, so pack comfortable walking shoes. The cobblestone streets and varied terrain make sturdy footwear essential for exploring the city's attractions.

- *Weather-Appropriate Clothing*: Check the weather forecast before your trip and pack accordingly. Layers are advisable, especially in spring and autumn, as temperatures can fluctuate throughout the day.

Visa and Entry Requirements

Before traveling to Ghent, it's important to be aware of the visa and entry requirements based on your nationality:

- *Schengen Area*: Belgium is part of the Schengen Agreement, allowing travelers from many countries to enter without a visa for short stays (up to 90 days) for tourism or business purposes. This includes citizens from the EU, the USA, Canada, Australia, and several other countries. Ensure your passport is valid for at least three months beyond your intended departure date.

- *Visa Requirements*: If you are not from a visa-exempt country, you will need to apply for a Schengen Visa. This typically involves submitting an application form, proof of accommodation, travel insurance, and evidence of sufficient funds for your stay. Applications should be made at the Belgian consulate or embassy in your country.

- *COVID-19 Regulations:* As regulations may change, check for any COVID-19 related entry requirements or travel restrictions before your trip. These may include vaccination proof, testing requirements, or quarantine measures.

- **Customs Regulations**: Familiarize yourself with Belgium's customs regulations regarding what you can bring into the country. This includes limits on alcohol, tobacco, and other goods.

summary

Planning your trip to Ghent involves careful consideration of the best time to visit, how long to stay, and ensuring you have the essentials covered. By understanding the local culture and travel requirements, you can make the most of your experience in this enchanting city. The following chapters will guide you through the many facets of Ghent, ensuring a memorable adventure awaits you.

CHAPTER 3: GETTING TO GHENT

Credit@google

Traveling to Ghent is convenient, thanks to its well-connected transportation network. Whether you are arriving by air, train, or car, this chapter provides essential information to help you navigate your journey to this beautiful city.

Arriving by Air

Brussels Airport (BRU) is the main international gateway for travelers coming to Ghent. Located approximately 60 kilometers (37 miles) from the city center, it is well-served by airlines from around the world.

- **Transportation from Brussels Airport to Ghent:**
  - Train: The most efficient way to travel from Brussels Airport to Ghent is by train. Direct trains

leave from the airport station to Ghent approximately every 30 minutes, with a journey time of about 30-40 minutes. Tickets can be purchased at ticket machines or online.

- Bus: Several bus companies operate from the airport to various destinations, including Ghent. However, this option may take longer than the train.

- Taxi/Ride-Sharing: Taxis are available at the airport, and ride-sharing services like Uber are also operational. The drive to Ghent takes approximately 50-60 minutes, depending on traffic conditions.

Antwerp International Airport (ANR) is another option for travelers, although it primarily serves regional flights. It is about 60 kilometers (37 miles) from Ghent.

- *Transportation from Antwerp Airport:*

- Train: From Antwerp, take a taxi or bus to the central station, and then catch a train to Ghent.

- Taxi/Ride-Sharing: Direct taxis can be hired, but this can be a more expensive option compared to public transport.

Arriving by Train

Ghent is well-connected by rail, making it an accessible destination for travelers arriving from other Belgian cities and neighboring countries. The main train station, Gent-Sint-Pieters, is located just outside the city center and serves both local and international routes.

- *Traveling from Major Cities*:

- Brussels: Direct trains run frequently from Brussels Central Station to Gent-Sint-Pieters, with a journey time of about 30 minutes.

- Bruges: Trains from Bruges to Ghent take approximately 30 minutes and operate regularly throughout the day.

- Antwerp: A direct train from Antwerp to Ghent takes about 40 minutes.

- Reaching the City Center: Upon arriving at Gent-Sint-Pieters station, you can easily reach the city center by tram, bus, or taxi. The tram ride to the city center takes around 30 minutes.

Arriving by Car

If you prefer to drive, Ghent is accessible via major highways:

- *From Brussels:* Take the E40 highway towards Ostend and exit at Ghent. The drive typically takes about an hour, depending on traffic conditions.

- *From Bruges*: The drive from Bruges takes around 30-40 minutes via the E40.

- *From Antwerp:* The journey from Antwerp to Ghent via the E17 takes approximately 40-50 minutes.

Parking in Ghent: The city has several parking facilities, including underground parking and park-and-ride options on the outskirts. Note that Ghent has a low-emission zone (LEZ), so ensure your vehicle complies with local regulations to avoid fines.

Public Transportation

Ghent boasts a reliable public transportation system that makes it easy to navigate the city:

- **Trams and Buses:** The city is serviced by a network of trams and buses operated by De Lijn. The tram system is especially convenient for reaching key attractions from the city center.

- **Tickets**: Tickets can be purchased at vending machines located at tram stops or on buses. A single ticket is valid for one hour and can be used on both trams and buses during that time.

- *City Card*: For those planning extensive travel within the city, consider purchasing a Gentse City Card, which offers unlimited access to public transport and entry to various attractions.

Taxi and Ride-Sharing Options

Taxis and ride-sharing services are widely available in Ghent, providing convenient options for getting around the city.

- **Taxis**: Taxis can be hailed on the street or booked via phone. They are generally safe and reliable, but fares can be higher than public transport.

- Ride-Sharing Services: Services like Uber operate in Ghent, offering a convenient and often cost-effective alternative to traditional taxis. You can book a ride using the app, and prices are generally transparent and competitive.

summary

Getting to Ghent is straightforward, whether you arrive by air, train, or car. The city's excellent transportation links and public transit options make it easy to explore both Ghent and its surroundings. With this chapter, you are equipped with all the necessary information to embark on your journey to discover the wonders of Ghent.

CHAPTER 4:

ACCOMMODATION

Credit@google

Finding the right place to stay is crucial to your travel experience in Ghent. The city offers a wide range of accommodation options to suit every budget and preference, from luxurious hotels to charming hostels. This chapter will guide you through the best options available in Ghent.

Top Hotels

Ghent boasts a variety of high-quality hotels that provide excellent service and amenities. Here are some of the top-rated hotels in the city:

- **Pillows Grand Boutique Reylof Ghent**: Housed in a former 18th-century palace, this hotel combines elegance with modern comfort. Guests can enjoy luxurious rooms, a spa, and an on-site restaurant serving gourmet cuisine. Its central location makes it an ideal base for exploring the city.

- *Hotel Harmony*: Located along the canals, this hotel offers stunning views of the water and a tranquil atmosphere. The rooms are spacious and well-appointed, and the hotel features a rooftop terrace, fitness center, and an excellent restaurant.

- *Hotel Amadeus*: Situated in the heart of Ghent, Hotel Amadeus is known for its charming decor and warm hospitality. Guests can enjoy a complimentary breakfast and easy access to nearby attractions.

Luxury Stays

For those seeking an indulgent experience, Ghent offers several luxurious accommodations:

- **Hotel Dukes' Palace Ghent:** A former ducal residence, this 5-star hotel is renowned for its opulent design and impeccable service. Guests can enjoy beautifully decorated rooms, a lush garden, a wellness area, and a fine dining restaurant. The hotel is conveniently located near major attractions.

- **The Francis Hotel**: This boutique hotel features modern, stylish rooms and exceptional service. Guests can relax in the elegant lounge or enjoy a meal at the on-site restaurant, which focuses on local and seasonal ingredients.

- *Sandton Grand Hotel Reylof Ghent:* Combining classic elegance with contemporary amenities, this luxury hotel features spacious rooms, a wellness center, and an exquisite restaurant. Its location allows easy access to both the city center and popular tourist sites.

Mid-Range Hotels

Travelers on a moderate budget can find numerous mid-range options that offer comfort and quality:

- *Hotel de Flandre*: This charming hotel is located in a historic building and features beautifully decorated rooms with a classic feel. Guests appreciate the convenient location and excellent breakfast offerings.

- *Ibis Styles Gent*: Known for its modern and quirky decor, this hotel provides a comfortable stay with a focus on affordability. It offers free breakfast, complimentary Wi-Fi, and a cozy atmosphere.

- *Hotel Castel*: A great choice for families and groups, Hotel Castel provides spacious rooms and a friendly atmosphere. Its location allows easy access to public transport, making it a convenient option for exploring the city.

Budget-Friendly Options

For travelers seeking affordable accommodations, Ghent has several budget-friendly options that do not compromise on quality:

- **Hostel Uppelink**: This lively hostel is situated along the river and offers both private and shared dormitory rooms. Guests can enjoy a communal kitchen, a bar, and organized events, making it a great place to meet fellow travelers.

- **Couchsurfing**: For those looking for a unique experience, consider Couchsurfing, where you can stay with local hosts for free. This option allows for cultural exchange and can provide valuable insights into Ghent's local life.

- **_Hotel Ibis Budget Gent_**: This hotel offers no-frills accommodations at a reasonable price. Rooms are clean and functional, making it a suitable choice for budget travelers who need a comfortable place to rest.

Current Prices

Accommodation prices in Ghent vary depending on the season, location, and type of accommodation. Here's a general overview of what you can expect:

- **_Luxury Hotels_**: Prices for luxury hotels typically range from €150 to €350 per night, with premium suites going higher during peak seasons.

- **_Mid-Range Hotels_**: Expect to pay between €80 and €150 per night for mid-range options, which often include breakfast.

- **_Budget-Friendly Options_**: Hostel prices generally start at around €20 for dormitory beds and range from €50 to €100 for private rooms. Budget hotels can be found in the €50 to €80 range.

- *Seasonal Variations*: Be mindful that prices can increase during peak tourist seasons (spring and summer) and during major events or festivals. Booking in advance is recommended to secure the best rates.

summary

Ghent offers a diverse range of accommodation options to meet the needs of every traveler. Whether you are looking for luxury, comfort, or budget-friendly stays, you will find suitable choices to enhance your experience in this vibrant city. As you plan your trip, consider your preferences and budget to select the perfect home base for your Ghent adventure.

CHAPTER 5: EXPLORING THE ATTRACTIONS

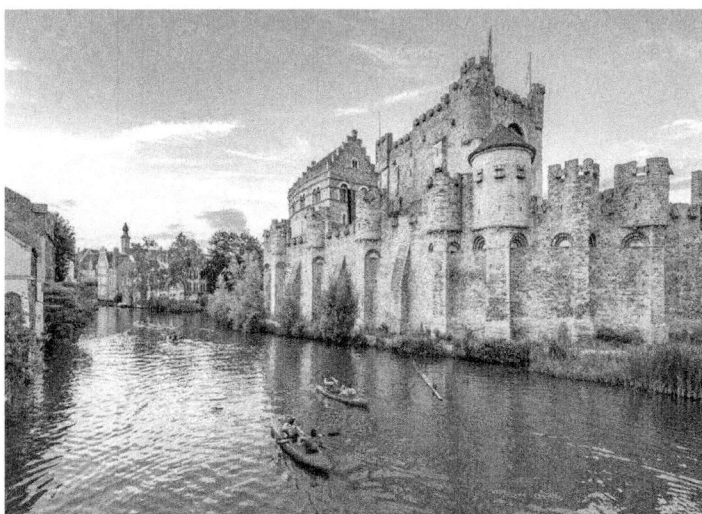

Credit@google

Ghent is a city rich in history, culture, and stunning architecture. This chapter provides a detailed overview of the city's top attractions, including key highlights, operational hours, entry fees, age requirements, and interesting facts to enhance your visit.

Summary Highlights

Ghent boasts a variety of attractions that cater to different interests. Here are some must-visit highlights:

- *Gravensteen Castle*: This medieval castle, also known as the Castle of the Counts, offers visitors a glimpse into Ghent's feudal past. Explore its towers, dungeons, and museum exhibits.

- **Saint Bavo's Cathedral**: Home to the famous Ghent Altarpiece, this Gothic cathedral is a masterpiece of art and architecture. Visitors can admire its stunning stained glass windows and intricate altar.

- **Museum of Fine Arts (MSK):** This museum houses an impressive collection of Flemish and Belgian art, featuring works by renowned artists such as Van Eyck and Rubens.

- **Patershol**: A historic district known for its cobbled streets and charming restaurants, Patershol is the perfect place to wander and discover local cuisine.

- *Graslei and Korenlei*: These picturesque streets along the riverbank are lined with beautiful medieval buildings and are ideal for a scenic stroll or a relaxing meal at a riverside café.

Operation Hours

Most attractions in Ghent operate year-round, but it's essential to check their specific opening hours, especially during holidays. Here are the general operating hours for key attractions:

- *Gravensteen Castle*:
  - Open daily from 10:00 AM to 6:00 PM

- Extended hours during peak tourist season (April to October).

- Saint Bavo's Cathedral:

- Open Monday to Saturday from 8:30 AM to 6:00 PM
- Sundays from 1:00 PM to 5:00 PM

- Museum of Fine Arts (MSK):

- Open Tuesday to Sunday from 10:00 AM to 6:00 PM
- Closed on Mondays

- Patershol and Graslei/Korenlei:

- These areas are open year-round and accessible at all hours, but dining establishments may have varying hours.

Entry Fees

Entry fees vary depending on the attraction. Here are some typical costs for popular sites:

- ***Gravensteen Castle***:
  - Adults: €12
  - Students/Seniors: €10
  - Children under 12: Free

- ***Saint Bavo's Cathedral***:

- Entry to the cathedral is free; however, there is a fee of €4 to view the Ghent Altarpiece.

- Museum of Fine Arts (MSK):

- Adults: €10

- Students/Seniors: €8

- Free for children under 18

- Patershol:

- Free to explore; dining costs vary by restaurant.

Age Requirements

Most attractions in Ghent are family-friendly, but some may have age-specific guidelines:

- *Gravensteen Castle*:

- Children are welcome, but adult supervision is required in certain areas due to steep stairs and heights.

- *Saint Bavo's Cathedral*:

- No age restrictions; the cathedral is accessible for all visitors.

- *Museum of Fine Arts (MSK):*

- Families with children are encouraged to visit, and special workshops are often available for younger visitors.

- *Dining in Patershol:*

- Most restaurants are family-friendly, but some may have age restrictions for evening dining or specific events.

Interesting Facts

Enhance your visit with these intriguing tidbits about Ghent's attractions:

- **Gravensteen Castle**: The castle's walls are over 800 years old, and it was once used as a prison. Today, it features life-sized wax figures that depict medieval life.

- *Saint Bavo's Cathedral*: The Ghent Altarpiece, painted by Jan van Eyck in the early 15th century, is considered one of the most important masterpieces of Northern Renaissance art and was famously stolen during World War II.

- *Museum of Fine Arts (MSK):* The museum not only houses remarkable artworks but also hosts temporary exhibitions that focus on various themes and artists.

- *Patershol*: This district was once a poor neighborhood but has since transformed into a trendy area filled with restaurants and art galleries. The name "Patershol" refers to the many monasteries that once existed there.

- *Graslei and Korenlei*: The buildings along these streets were once home to merchants and traders, and they showcase a mix of architectural styles, including Gothic and Renaissance.

summary

Ghent's attractions offer a rich tapestry of history, art, and culture, making it a captivating destination for travelers. By exploring these highlights, you can immerse yourself in the city's unique charm and heritage. Remember to check the operational hours and entry fees before your visit to ensure a seamless experience.

CHAPTER 6: DINING AND CULINARY SCENE

Credit@google

Ghent is a culinary gem, offering a diverse range of dining options that reflect both local traditions and contemporary trends. From traditional Belgian dishes to innovative cuisine, this chapter will explore the local culinary scene, highlighting specialties, dining styles, and must-visit establishments.

Local Cuisine and Specialties

Ghent's culinary landscape is rich with flavors and traditions, shaped by its history and geography. Here are some local dishes and specialties you should try:

- *Waterzooi*: A signature dish of Ghent, waterzooi is a hearty stew made with fish or chicken, vegetables, and a creamy broth. This comforting meal is often served with crusty bread.

- *Gentse Stoverij*: This Flemish beef stew is slowly cooked in dark beer, resulting in tender meat and rich flavors. It's typically served with fries or mashed potatoes.

- *Grilled Eel:* A local delicacy, grilled eel is often served with a side of salad or potatoes. This dish highlights Ghent's proximity to waterways, where eels are abundant.

- *Bicky Burger*: A unique Belgian fast-food creation, the Bicky Burger features a spiced meat patty topped with a special sauce and served in a soft bun. It's a popular choice for a quick bite.

- **Cuberdon**: Also known as "neuzekes" (little noses), cuberdons are raspberry-flavored gummy sweets with a soft, gooey center. They make for a delightful local treat.

Fine Dining Restaurants

For those seeking a memorable dining experience, Ghent offers several fine dining options that showcase the best of Belgian and international cuisine:

- **_Restaurant Paul:_** Known for its exquisite seasonal dishes and elegant ambiance, Restaurant Paul focuses on using fresh, local ingredients to create refined culinary experiences. The tasting menu is highly recommended.

- **De Graslei**: Situated along the picturesque river, De Graslei offers a stunning setting and an impressive menu featuring classic Belgian dishes with a modern twist. The extensive wine list complements the dining experience beautifully.

- **_Ode_**: This Michelin-starred restaurant emphasizes creativity and quality. The menu features a mix of traditional Flemish ingredients and international flavors, presented in a contemporary style. Reservations are advisable.

- **Bistro de l'Eau d'Olle:** A charming bistro known for its relaxed atmosphere and exceptional cuisine, Bistro de l'Eau d'Olle serves seasonal dishes with a focus on local produce. The wine pairings enhance the overall dining experience.

Casual Eateries

For a more relaxed dining experience, Ghent is filled with casual eateries that offer delicious food at reasonable prices:

- **De Graslei Café:** A popular spot among locals, this café serves a variety of sandwiches, salads, and Belgian classics. Its riverside terrace is perfect for enjoying a meal on sunny days.

- **Café 't Klokhuys**: This cozy café offers a selection of light meals and local beers. It's an ideal spot to relax after exploring the city, with friendly service and a welcoming atmosphere.

- **Foodbox**: A trendy eatery that focuses on healthy, organic food, Foodbox offers a variety of bowls, wraps, and smoothies. It's perfect for a quick, nutritious meal on the go.

- ***Bakkerij F. Troupin***: This casual bakery specializes in traditional Belgian pastries and bread. Stop by for a delicious croissant or a slice of cake to accompany your coffee.

Cafés and Bakeries

Ghent's café culture is vibrant, with many places offering a cozy atmosphere to enjoy coffee and pastries:

- ***Café Labath***: Renowned for its artisanal coffee, Café Labath is a must-visit for coffee lovers. The café serves expertly brewed espresso and filter coffee, along with a selection of pastries and light snacks.

- *Patisserie P. De Clercq*: This charming patisserie offers a wide range of cakes, tarts, and chocolates. Don't miss their signature dessert, the "Gentse Neuzen," a local favorite.

- *Café Bouno*: A delightful spot for breakfast or brunch, Café Bouno offers a variety of options, from freshly baked pastries to hearty breakfast bowls. The warm ambiance makes it a great place to start your day.

- *Mokabon*: A historic café that has been serving locals since 1928, Mokabon is known for its traditional hot chocolate and delightful pastries.

The cozy interior is perfect for a quiet afternoon break.

Street Food

Ghent's street food scene is thriving, with various options to satisfy your cravings while exploring the city:

- **Frituur**: No visit to Ghent is complete without indulging in Belgian fries. Frituur (fry stands) can be found throughout the city, serving crispy fries with a variety of tasty sauces, including the classic mayonnaise, and special house sauces.

- *Food Trucks:* Look out for food trucks scattered around popular areas, offering everything from gourmet burgers to falafel wraps. These mobile kitchens serve delicious meals at affordable prices.

- *Market Stalls*: During the weekends, local markets pop up throughout the city, where vendors sell a range of street food options, from fresh seafood to artisanal cheeses. These markets are a great way to taste local flavors.

- *Burgers and Waffles on the Go*: Several street vendors specialize in classic Belgian waffles and burgers, allowing you to grab a quick bite as you explore the city. Look for waffle carts where you can enjoy a warm, freshly made waffle topped with your choice of syrup, fruits, or whipped cream.

summary

Ghent's dining scene is a celebration of flavors, creativity, and tradition. From fine dining establishments to casual eateries and street food stalls, there's something to satisfy every palate. Embrace the local cuisine, explore new flavors, and enjoy the culinary delights that Ghent has to offer.

CHAPTER 7: SHOPPING IN GHENT

Credit@google

Ghent offers a vibrant shopping scene that combines contemporary retail with historic charm. Whether you're seeking high-end fashion, unique souvenirs, or local artisan goods, this chapter explores the best shopping districts, markets, and shops in the city.

Popular Shopping Districts

Ghent's shopping districts are a blend of traditional and modern, featuring everything from chic boutiques to large retail stores. Here are some of the key areas to explore:

- *Veldstraat*: Known as Ghent's premier shopping street, Veldstraat is lined with a mix of international brands and local boutiques. Here, you'll find everything from high-end fashion to unique gifts, making it a must-visit for any shopper.

- **Sint-Baafsplein**: This square is not only famous for the stunning Saint Bavo's Cathedral but also for its surrounding shops. Enjoy a leisurely stroll while browsing local boutiques and cafés that offer a delightful selection of goods.

- **Kouter**: A beautiful square known for its elegant architecture, Kouter features upscale shops and fine dining. The area is also home to a flower market on weekends, adding to its charm.

- **Patershol**: This historic district is filled with quaint shops and boutiques that specialize in unique gifts, home décor, and fashion. The narrow streets and medieval buildings make shopping here a delightful experience.

Local Markets

Ghent's markets are a fantastic way to experience local culture and find fresh produce, crafts, and specialties. Here are some notable markets to visit:

- *Saturday Market (Sint-Pietersplein):* Held every Saturday morning, this bustling market offers a wide array of fresh fruits, vegetables, cheese, and local delicacies. It's the perfect place to mingle with locals and taste regional specialties.

- ***Flower Market (Kouter):*** Every Sunday morning, Kouter transforms into a vibrant flower market, where vendors sell fresh flowers, plants, and gardening supplies. It's a lovely way to spend a Sunday and pick up some beautiful blooms.

- ***Mercatorkwartier***: This lively market offers a variety of local products, including artisanal foods, handmade crafts, and vintage goods. It's a great spot to find unique items and support local artisans.

- ***Christmas Market***: If visiting during the holiday season, don't miss the Christmas market in the city center. The market features beautifully decorated stalls selling handmade gifts, festive treats, and mulled wine.

Souvenir Shopping

Bringing home a piece of Ghent is easy with its wide range of unique souvenirs. Here are some popular options:

- **Cuberdons**: Known as "neuzekes," these raspberry-flavored gummy sweets with a soft center are a local specialty. They make for a delightful and tasty souvenir to share with friends and family.

- *Ghent Altarpiece Replicas*: Miniature replicas of the famous Ghent Altarpiece are available at various souvenir shops. These artistic pieces are perfect for art lovers and those wishing to remember their visit to the cathedral.

- *Local Beer*: Belgium is famous for its beer, and Ghent is home to several breweries. Look for unique local brews to take home, many of which come in beautifully designed bottles.

- *Artisan Crafts:* Seek out shops selling handmade crafts, such as pottery, textiles, and jewelry. These items often reflect the local culture and make for meaningful gifts.

Artisan Shops

Ghent is home to many talented artisans who create unique products that showcase the city's craftsmanship. Here are some noteworthy artisan shops to explore:

- *De Hopduvel*: A local shop specializing in traditional Belgian products, De Hopduvel offers a wide range of artisanal foods, including chocolates, beers, and cheeses. It's a great place to find gourmet gifts.

- *Artisana*: This shop focuses on handmade crafts and artisanal goods, including pottery, textiles, and home décor. Each item reflects the skill and creativity of local artisans, making it a perfect spot for unique gifts.

- **Rokoko**: A boutique that specializes in vintage clothing and accessories, Rokoko features a curated selection of one-of-a-kind pieces that are perfect for fashion enthusiasts looking for something special.

- **Bureau M**: This design shop showcases the work of local artists and designers, offering a variety of contemporary home décor, art prints, and fashion accessories. Supporting local talent has never been easier.

summary

Shopping in Ghent offers an enriching experience that combines local culture, history, and creativity. Whether you're wandering through bustling markets, exploring charming artisan shops, or picking up unique souvenirs, you'll find plenty of opportunities to discover the city's unique flair. Embrace the local shopping scene and take home a piece of Ghent that reflects its vibrant spirit.

CHAPTER 8: NIGHTLIFE AND ENTERTAINMENT

Credit@google

Ghent comes alive at night, offering a dynamic nightlife scene that caters to all tastes, whether you're in the mood for a cozy bar, an exhilarating live music venue, or a vibrant nightclub. This chapter delves into the best places for nightlife and entertainment in Ghent, ensuring you experience the city's energetic after-dark atmosphere.

Bars and Pubs

Ghent boasts a diverse range of bars and pubs, each with its unique ambiance and drink offerings. Here are some popular spots to unwind and enjoy a drink:

- **Dulle Griet**: This iconic pub is famous for its extensive selection of Belgian beers, with over 300 varieties on the menu. The quirky interior and friendly atmosphere make it a favorite among locals and tourists alike. Don't forget to try the house specialty, the "Dulle Griet" beer, served in a unique glass.

- *Het Waterhuis aan de Bierkant*: Situated along the scenic riverbanks, this bar offers a fantastic view and a cozy atmosphere. With a vast selection of local brews and knowledgeable staff, it's an excellent place to discover new flavors while enjoying the picturesque setting.

- *Pakhuis*: Located in a former warehouse, Pakhuis combines a lively bar with a restaurant. The extensive drink menu features a wide range of Belgian beers and cocktails, and the unique industrial décor adds to its charm. It's a great spot for both drinks and a hearty meal.

- *The Monk*: A laid-back pub with a welcoming vibe, The Monk is known for its relaxed atmosphere and friendly service. It serves a variety of local beers and offers a small menu of tasty snacks, making it perfect for a casual night out.

Live Music Venues

For music enthusiasts, Ghent offers a variety of venues hosting live performances across different genres. Here are some top spots to catch a show:

- *Vooruit*: This cultural center is a hub for music, theater, and art. It hosts a wide range of live music events, from indie bands to international acts. The venue itself is an architectural gem, providing a unique backdrop for unforgettable performances.

- *Charlatan*: A popular live music venue in the heart of Ghent, Charlatan features a mix of local and international artists across various genres, including rock, jazz, and electronic music. The intimate setting creates a vibrant atmosphere, making it a go-to spot for music lovers.

- *Café de Grote Vriendelijke*: This cozy café often hosts open mic nights and local band performances. The relaxed ambiance and friendly crowd make it a great place to discover emerging talent and enjoy live music.

- **Oude Vleeshuis:** A historic venue that hosts classical music concerts and special events, Oude Vleeshuis provides a unique cultural experience. The beautiful setting enhances the enjoyment of live performances.

Cultural Performances

Ghent's cultural scene is rich and varied, with many opportunities to experience theater, dance, and art. Here are some notable venues to explore:

- *KVS (Koninklijke Vlaamse Schouwburg):*
This theater focuses on contemporary performances and often showcases innovative works from local and international artists. From drama to dance, KVS offers a diverse program that reflects the cultural pulse of Ghent.

- *De Bijloke*: A renowned concert hall and cultural venue, De Bijloke hosts a variety of performances, including classical concerts, contemporary music, and dance shows. The stunning setting adds to the allure of the performances held here.

- *Theater Arena*: This theater features an array of performances, including local productions, international tours, and experimental works. The intimate setting allows for a close connection between performers and the audience.

- *Festival van Vlaanderen:* If you're visiting in the spring or fall, be sure to check out this annual festival celebrating classical music, opera, and theater. It showcases talented artists from around the world and offers a range of performances in various venues across the city.

Nightclubs and Entertainment Spots

For those looking to dance the night away or enjoy vibrant entertainment, Ghent has several nightclubs and entertainment venues to explore:

- **Club 69**: Known for its energetic atmosphere and eclectic music selection, Club 69 is one of Ghent's top nightclubs. It features local and international DJs, hosting themed nights and events that keep the dance floor packed until the early hours.

- **Decadance**: This popular nightclub is renowned for its lively parties and diverse music styles, including electronic, techno, and pop. With a spacious dance floor and a stylish bar, it's a favorite spot for both locals and visitors.

- **Café d'Anvers**: A legendary club located in a former church, Café d'Anvers offers an unforgettable nightlife experience. With its unique setting and top-notch DJs, it draws a vibrant crowd eager to dance the night away.

- *De Centrale*: A multi-purpose venue that combines a nightclub, concert hall, and cultural center, De Centrale hosts various events, from club nights to live performances. It's a great place to experience Ghent's dynamic nightlife and cultural scene.

summary

Ghent's nightlife and entertainment options cater to a wide range of preferences, ensuring there's something for everyone to enjoy. From cozy pubs and vibrant bars to dynamic live music venues and nightclubs, the city offers an array of experiences that capture its lively spirit. Whether you're seeking a laid-back evening with friends or an exhilarating night out, Ghent's nightlife scene will not disappoint.

CHAPTER 9: DAY TRIPS AND NEARBY DESTINATIONS

Credit@google

Ghent is ideally located for exploring some of Belgium's most captivating cities and natural landscapes. This chapter highlights top day trip options and nearby destinations that offer a diverse array of experiences, from historic architecture to stunning coastlines.

Bruges

Distance from Ghent: Approximately 30 km (18 miles)

Bruges, often referred to as the "Venice of the North," is a UNESCO World Heritage site known for its picturesque canals, medieval buildings, and cobblestone streets.

- What to See: Must-visit attractions include the Belfry of Bruges, where you can climb for panoramic views, the Markt square with its colorful facades, and the Basilica of the Holy Blood, which houses a revered relic. Don't miss the scenic canal boat tours for a unique perspective of the city.

- Activities: Bruges is perfect for a leisurely stroll, allowing visitors to immerse themselves in its charming atmosphere. Enjoy local specialties like Flemish stew and Bruges' famous chocolates in the many cafés and eateries.

- Getting There: Bruges is easily accessible from Ghent by train, with frequent connections taking around 30 minutes. Alternatively, a drive takes about 40 minutes.

Antwerp

Distance from Ghent: Approximately 60 km (37 miles)

Antwerp, Belgium's second-largest city, is renowned for its fashion scene, vibrant arts culture, and historic architecture.

- What to See: Visit the impressive Cathedral of Our Lady, a UNESCO World Heritage site that houses masterpieces by Rubens. Explore the Antwerp Zoo, the fashion district, and the historic Diamond Quarter. The Museum aan de Stroom (MAS) offers stunning views and exhibitions about the city's maritime history.

- Activities: Antwerp is a shopper's paradise, with everything from high-end boutiques to vintage shops. The city also boasts a lively nightlife, particularly in the trendy neighborhoods of Zuid and Het Eilandje.

- Getting There: Trains from Ghent to Antwerp run frequently, with a travel time of about 50 minutes. Driving takes roughly an hour, making it a convenient day trip option.

The Belgian Coast

Distance from Ghent: Varies by destination; the closest coastal city, Oostende, is about 45 km (28 miles)

The Belgian Coast offers a refreshing escape with its sandy beaches, charming seaside towns, and vibrant promenade life.

- What to See: Oostende is a popular choice, known for its beachside attractions and the historic Fort Napoleon. The town features a lively harbor and numerous seafood restaurants. Other coastal towns worth visiting include Knokke-Heist, renowned for its upscale shops and art galleries, and Blankenberge, known for its bustling beach and pier.

- Activities: Enjoy beach activities, bike along the coast, or relax in one of the many beach clubs. Coastal towns often host festivals and events, particularly in the summer months.

- Getting There: Direct trains from Ghent to Oostende take about 30 minutes, making it an easy day trip. Biking along the coast is also a popular option, with designated paths connecting various towns.

Nature Parks

For those seeking outdoor adventures and natural beauty, several parks near Ghent provide opportunities for hiking, biking, and exploring diverse landscapes.

- ***Bourgoyen-Ossemeersen Nature Reserve***: Located just a few kilometers from the city center, this nature reserve is a haven for birdwatchers and nature lovers. The park features several walking trails that wind through wetlands and meadows, offering opportunities to spot various bird species.

- ***Langevelde Nature Reserve***: A tranquil area perfect for hiking and picnicking, Langevelde offers a peaceful escape with beautiful scenery and wildlife. The park's trails are well-marked, making it accessible for visitors of all ages.

- *Gravensteen Castle Park*: Combining history and nature, the park surrounding Ghent's Gravensteen Castle is a lovely place to wander. The gardens and pathways offer a picturesque setting, with the castle providing a dramatic backdrop.

- *Hoge Kempen National Park*: About 100 km (62 miles) from Ghent, this national park is worth the drive for its stunning landscapes, including heathlands, forests, and diverse wildlife. It offers numerous trails for hiking and biking, as well as picnic areas for a leisurely day in nature.

summary

Ghent's prime location allows for a variety of enriching day trips and nearby destinations, making it an ideal base for exploring Belgium. Whether you're drawn to the historical charm of Bruges and Antwerp, the refreshing breeze of the Belgian Coast, or the tranquility of nature parks, each destination offers its unique experiences. Embrace the opportunity to discover the diverse beauty of the region surrounding Ghent, creating lasting memories on your travels.

CHAPTER 10: PRACTICAL TIPS

Traveling to a new city can be an exciting adventure, but it also comes with its own set of challenges. This chapter provides essential practical tips to help you navigate Ghent smoothly, from language and currency to safety considerations and local etiquette.

Language and Communication

Belgium is a multilingual country, with three official languages: Dutch, French, and German. In

Ghent, the primary language spoken is Dutch (specifically, the Flemish dialect), but you'll find that many locals also speak English, especially in tourist areas.

- *Common Phrases*: While most people in Ghent understand English, learning a few basic Dutch phrases can enhance your experience. Here are some useful phrases:

- Hello: Hallo

- Thank you: Dank u wel (formal) / Bedankt (informal)

- Please: Alstublieft

- Excuse me: Pardon

- Do you speak English?: Spreekt u Engels?

- *Communication Tips:* When communicating, it's always appreciated if you make an effort to speak the local language. If you're not fluent in Dutch, starting with a friendly "Hello" in Dutch and then switching to English is a polite approach. Many locals are accommodating and will happily switch languages if they see you're trying.

Currency and Payment

Belgium uses the Euro (€) as its official currency, with notes available in denominations of 5, 10, 20, 50, 100, 200, and 500, and coins in 1, 2, 5, 10, 20, and 50 cents, as well as 1 and 2 euros.

- *Currency Exchange*: Currency exchange services are available at banks, airports, and exchange offices. It's advisable to exchange money at banks for better rates. ATMs are widely available, and they accept international debit and credit cards.

- *Payment Methods*: Credit and debit cards are widely accepted in Ghent, especially Visa and Mastercard. However, some smaller shops, cafés, and markets may prefer cash. It's wise to carry a small amount of cash for purchases at these locations.

- *Tipping*: Tipping in Belgium is not mandatory, but it is appreciated. In restaurants, it's common to round up the bill or leave a small tip (around

5-10%) for good service. In cafés and bars, leaving small change is customary.

Safety Considerations

Ghent is generally considered a safe city for travelers, but like any urban area, it's essential to take standard safety precautions.

- *Personal Safety*: Be aware of your surroundings, especially in crowded areas or on public transport. Avoid displaying valuable items, such as expensive jewelry or electronics, to minimize the risk of theft.

- *Emergency Contacts:* In case of emergencies, dial 112 for police, fire, or medical assistance. It's also helpful to have the contact information for your country's embassy or consulate.

- *Health Precautions*: Ensure you have adequate travel insurance that covers health emergencies. While Belgium has a high standard of healthcare, it's always best to be prepared. Consider bringing any necessary medications, and check if you need vaccinations before traveling.

Local Etiquette

Understanding local customs and etiquette can enrich your travel experience in Ghent and help you connect with locals.

- *Greetings*: A handshake is the standard greeting in Belgium. In more informal settings, you may also encounter cheek kissing (usually two kisses) among friends and acquaintances, starting with the left cheek.

- *Dining Etiquette*: When dining, wait for the host to start the meal before beginning to eat. It's polite to keep your hands on the table (but not your elbows) while eating. If you're invited to someone's home, it's customary to bring a small gift, such as flowers or chocolates.

- *Public Behavior*: Belgians generally value politeness and personal space. Avoid loud conversations in public places and respect local customs. It's customary to say "Hello" when entering a shop and "Goodbye" when leaving.

- *Dress Code*: Belgians tend to dress well, especially in urban areas. While casual attire is acceptable, consider dressing up slightly when visiting fine dining restaurants or cultural events.

summary

By keeping these practical tips in mind, you can navigate Ghent with confidence and make the most of your visit. Understanding the local language, currency, safety measures, and etiquette will enhance your experience and allow you to engage more meaningfully with the city and its residents. Enjoy your adventure in Ghent, a city that beautifully blends history, culture, and vibrant life!

CHAPTER 11: ITINERARY IDEAS

Credit@google

Exploring Ghent can be an enriching experience for travelers of all types. Whether you're visiting with family, seeking cultural experiences, or indulging in the local culinary scene, this chapter provides tailored itinerary ideas to help you maximize your time in the city.

Family-Friendly Itinerary

Day 1: Exploring Ghent's History and Culture

- Morning: Begin your adventure at Gravensteen Castle. Explore the medieval fortress and learn about its history. Children will enjoy the interactive exhibits and the chance to climb the towers for panoramic views of the city.

- Lunch: Head to De Graslei for lunch at a family-friendly café or restaurant that offers outdoor seating and kid-friendly menus.

- Afternoon: Visit the STAM - Ghent City Museum, where kids can engage with interactive displays and learn about the city's evolution through time. The museum has specific sections designed for children.

- Evening: Take a stroll along the Graslei and Korenlei. Enjoy the beautiful scenery along the river and consider a family dinner at a nearby restaurant with local cuisine.

Day 2: Nature and Adventure
- Morning: Spend the day at Bourgoyen-Ossemeersen Nature Reserve. Enjoy

walking trails suitable for all ages and bring a picnic to enjoy in the natural surroundings.

- Lunch: Pack a picnic or visit a local eatery nearby.

- Afternoon: Head to the Ghent Zoo, located close to the city center. It offers a range of animals and interactive exhibits, perfect for an engaging family experience.

- Evening: Finish your day with a boat tour along Ghent's canals, offering a unique perspective of the city, with commentary about its history and landmarks.

Cultural and Historical Itinerary

Day 1: Discovering Ghent's Artistic Heritage

- Morning: Start at the Museum of Fine Arts (MSK) to explore its collection of Flemish art, including works by Van Eyck and Rubens. Don't miss the nearby S.M.A.K., showcasing contemporary art.

- Lunch: Enjoy lunch at Pakhuis, a trendy restaurant that serves local dishes with a modern twist.

- Afternoon: Visit the St. Bavo's Cathedral, home to the famous painting "The Adoration of the Mystic

Lamb" by the Van Eyck brothers. The cathedral's stunning architecture is also a highlight.

- Evening: Explore the Patershol district, a historic area filled with narrow streets and charming houses. Choose a restaurant here for dinner, immersing yourself in the local atmosphere.

Day 2: Embracing History

- Morning: Begin with a visit to Gravensteen Castle to delve into Ghent's medieval past. Participate in guided tours that often include engaging storytelling.

- Lunch: Dine at De Graslei, enjoying riverside views while tasting traditional Belgian dishes.

- Afternoon: Walk to Belfry of Ghent and climb the tower for stunning views of the city. Afterward, explore the City Hall, noted for its stunning Gothic and Renaissance architecture.

- Evening: Enjoy an evening performance at the Ghent Opera House or check for local concerts and cultural events happening during your visit.

Food and Drink Itinerary

Day 1: Local Delights
- Morning: Start your day with breakfast at Le Pain Quotidien, known for its organic pastries and

breads. Enjoy a leisurely meal with fresh coffee and local specialties.

- Mid-Morning: Visit the Ghent Market for fresh produce and local goods. It's a great way to experience the local culture and perhaps pick up ingredients for a picnic.

- Lunch: Head to Osteria, a renowned spot for traditional Italian dishes prepared with local ingredients. Try their pasta, which is made fresh daily.

- Afternoon: Participate in a chocolate-making workshop at a local chocolatier, where you can learn about the art of Belgian chocolate and create your own treats.

- Evening: Enjoy dinner at De Graslei, where you can sample traditional Belgian dishes like carbonnade flamande (beef stew) and enjoy a local beer.

Day 2: Culinary Exploration

- Morning: Begin your day with a visit to Brouwerij Gruut, a local brewery where you can take a tour and sample unique craft beers brewed on-site.

- Lunch: Experience a casual lunch at De Foyer, known for its delicious brunch options, including waffles and savory dishes.

- Afternoon: Take a food tour that explores local markets, street food, and iconic Belgian dishes. This is a great way to discover hidden culinary gems in the city.

- Evening: Conclude your culinary journey with a dinner reservation at Hertog Jan, a Michelin-starred restaurant that focuses on innovative dishes using seasonal ingredients. Be sure to book in advance to secure your table.

summary

These itinerary ideas cater to various interests, allowing you to experience Ghent's rich history, family-friendly attractions, and vibrant culinary scene. Whether you're traveling with family, seeking cultural immersion, or indulging in the local flavors, each itinerary offers a unique perspective on this beautiful city. Enjoy your adventures in Ghent!

CHAPTER 12: GETTING AROUND

Credit@google

Navigating Ghent is a straightforward and enjoyable experience, thanks to its well-connected public transportation system, bike-friendly infrastructure, and walkable streets. This chapter provides an overview of various transportation options to help you explore the city efficiently.

Public Transportation Options

Ghent boasts an efficient public transportation network, making it easy to reach various attractions and neighborhoods.

- *Trams*: The tram system is operated by De Lijn and connects the city center with surrounding areas. Trams are a reliable option for traveling short distances within the city. Tickets can be purchased at vending machines or on board.

- **Buses**: Buses complement the tram network, providing access to areas that may not be served by trams. They are also operated by De Lijn and follow a similar ticketing system.

- **Tickets and Passes:** Tickets for public transportation can be purchased for single rides, or you can buy a day pass that allows unlimited travel for 24 hours. Consider purchasing a multi-day pass if you plan to use public transport frequently during your stay.

- **Schedule and Routes**: Timetables are available online and at tram/bus stops. Routes are clearly marked, and information is typically available in

English, making it easier for tourists to navigate the system.

Renting a Bike

Ghent is a bike-friendly city, and cycling is a popular way to explore its picturesque streets and scenic canals.

- ***Bike Rentals***: Various shops and rental services offer bicycles for rent, with options ranging from traditional bikes to electric bikes. Rentals can be hourly or daily, with many places providing discounts for longer rentals.

- ***Bike Sharing***: Lime and Donkey Republic offer bike-sharing services, allowing you to rent a bike via a mobile app. Simply locate a bike, unlock it, and enjoy your ride. Make sure to return it to a designated area.

- ***Cycling Infrastructure:*** Ghent has dedicated bike lanes throughout the city, ensuring safe travel for cyclists. Following local cycling rules and being mindful of pedestrians is essential while biking.

- ***Bike Tours:*** For those who prefer a guided experience, consider joining a bike tour that will take you through the city's highlights while providing insights into its history and culture.

Walking and Accessibility

Exploring Ghent on foot is an excellent way to soak in the city's charming atmosphere, beautiful architecture, and vibrant street life.

- **Walkability**: The city center is compact and pedestrian-friendly, making it easy to navigate on foot. Many attractions are within walking distance of one another, allowing you to explore at your own pace.

- **Walking Tours**: Guided walking tours are available, covering various themes such as historical sites, culinary delights, and local legends. These tours are an engaging way to learn about Ghent's culture and heritage.

- *Accessibility*: Ghent is generally accessible for individuals with mobility challenges, but some historical sites may have limited accessibility due to their age. Public transportation is equipped to accommodate wheelchair users, and many restaurants and shops offer accessible entrances.

- *Pavement and Pathways:* Sidewalks are well-maintained, and pedestrian crossings are marked. However, be mindful of cobblestone streets in some areas, which can be uneven and slippery in wet weather.

summary

Getting around Ghent is convenient and enjoyable, whether you prefer the ease of public transportation, the freedom of cycling, or the charm of exploring on foot. With its well-connected transport options and pedestrian-friendly environment, you'll have no trouble discovering all that this vibrant city has to offer.

CHAPTER 13: LOCAL EVENTS AND FESTIVALS

Credit@gooogle

Ghent is not only known for its stunning architecture and rich history but also for its vibrant cultural scene, which comes alive through a variety of local events and festivals throughout the year.

This chapter provides an overview of the annual calendar of events and notable festivals that showcase the city's unique traditions and lively atmosphere.

Annual Calendar of Events

Ghent hosts a wide array of events year-round, offering something for every type of visitor. Here's a month-by-month breakdown of key events:

- January

- Gentse Winterfeesten: A winter festival featuring a Christmas market, ice skating rink, and festive activities for families.

- *February*

   - Carnaval: Celebrated in various forms, the Ghent Carnival features parades, music, and colorful costumes, drawing locals and visitors alike.

- *March*

   - Art & Antiques Fair: An annual fair where collectors and art enthusiasts can discover antiques and art pieces from various eras.

- *April*

   - Gentse Feesten (Ghent Festival): A major cultural festival that takes place in mid-April, featuring performances, street artists, and local food.

- *May*

- Museum Night: A night of free access to various museums in Ghent, allowing visitors to explore exhibitions and enjoy special events.

- *June*

- Gent Jazz Festival: A renowned jazz festival attracting top international artists, set against the backdrop of the picturesque city.

- *July*

- Festival van de Jeugd: A youth festival featuring workshops, performances, and activities designed for younger audiences.

- *August*

- Boombalfestival: A lively festival dedicated to folk dance and music, featuring various workshops and performances in traditional dance styles.

- September

- Gentse Feesten: This festival celebrates local culture with concerts, street performances, and food stalls scattered throughout the city.

- October

- Film Fest Gent: A prestigious film festival showcasing a variety of films, including premieres and special screenings, attracting filmmakers and cinema lovers.

- November

- Food Festival: A culinary celebration highlighting local chefs and restaurants, with tastings, cooking demonstrations, and workshops.

- December

- Christmas Market: A festive market featuring local crafts, seasonal treats, and holiday decorations, transforming the city into a winter wonderland.

Notable Festivals and Celebrations

In addition to the annual events, Ghent is known for several key festivals that highlight the city's cultural richness and community spirit:

- *Gentse Feesten:*

- Occurring in mid-July, this is one of the largest cultural festivals in Belgium, lasting for ten days. It encompasses a diverse range of activities, including street performances, concerts, art exhibitions, and food stalls. The festival transforms the city into a vibrant celebration of arts and culture, drawing thousands of visitors each year.

- *Festival van Vlaanderen*:

- A classical music festival that takes place in various locations across Ghent, featuring performances by world-class orchestras, soloists, and chamber music ensembles. The festival typically runs from September to November, offering a rich program that celebrates both classical and contemporary music.

- Gentse Feesten (Ghent Festival):

- This festival celebrates the rich history and culture of Ghent with a focus on local artists and musicians. The streets are filled with vibrant decorations, food stalls, and activities for families, making it a must-visit event.

- Gent Jazz Festival:

- Held annually in July, this festival features a lineup of international and local jazz artists. It offers a mix of free outdoor concerts and ticketed performances, providing a platform for both established musicians and emerging talent.

- Film Fest Gent:

- Taking place in October, this renowned film festival attracts filmmakers, critics, and film enthusiasts from around the world. The festival screens a diverse selection of films, including international premieres, and often includes discussions and workshops with industry professionals.

- Midsummer Festival:

- Celebrated in late June, this festival marks the summer solstice with music, dance, and outdoor activities. It's a lively event that brings together locals and visitors to enjoy the warm weather and festive atmosphere.

summary

Ghent's local events and festivals provide a wonderful opportunity to engage with the city's culture, traditions, and community. Whether you're interested in music, art, food, or simply enjoying the festive atmosphere, there's always something happening in Ghent to enhance your visit. Be sure to check the local calendar during your stay to experience the vibrant spirit of this remarkable city.

CHAPTER 14:
SUSTAINABILITY AND
RESPONSIBLE TOURISM

Credit@google

As travelers become increasingly aware of their impact on the environment and local communities, Ghent stands out as a model city for sustainability and responsible tourism. This chapter explores the eco-friendly practices implemented in the city and how visitors can support local communities while enjoying their stay.

Eco-Friendly Practices

Ghent has taken significant strides toward sustainability, making it a leader in eco-friendly practices. Here are some key initiatives and practices to be aware of:

- Green Transportation:

- The city promotes the use of public transportation, cycling, and walking as primary modes of travel. Ghent is well-equipped with an extensive network of bike paths and pedestrian-friendly areas, making it easy for visitors to choose environmentally friendly options over cars.

- Electric vehicle charging stations are also available throughout the city for those who prefer to drive.

- *Sustainable Accommodation:*

- Many hotels and accommodations in Ghent are committed to sustainable practices, including energy-efficient systems, waste reduction programs, and sourcing local and organic products. Look for establishments that have eco-certifications, which indicate a commitment to sustainable tourism.

- *Waste Management and Recycling*:

- Ghent has implemented comprehensive waste management systems, encouraging residents and visitors to recycle and reduce waste. Public bins are clearly marked for different types of waste, making it easy to dispose of items properly.

- Many restaurants and shops have adopted policies to minimize single-use plastics, opting for biodegradable or recyclable materials instead.

- *Green Spaces:*

- The city is home to numerous parks and green areas that provide recreational spaces for both locals and visitors. These areas contribute to urban biodiversity and improve air quality, making Ghent a pleasant place to explore.

- Initiatives such as urban gardening projects promote local food production and environmental awareness.

- *Sustainable Food Practices:*

- Ghent is known for its emphasis on local, organic, and seasonal food. Many restaurants prioritize sourcing ingredients from local farms, reducing the carbon footprint associated with transportation.

- The city's "Veggie Day," where residents are encouraged to eat vegetarian meals, exemplifies Ghent's commitment to sustainable eating practices.

Supporting Local Communities

Responsible tourism goes beyond environmental practices; it also involves actively supporting the local economy and communities. Here are ways to engage in responsible tourism while in Ghent:

- *Choose Local Businesses*:

   - When dining, shopping, or seeking accommodations, opt for local businesses rather than international chains. This ensures that a higher percentage of your spending stays within the community, supporting local jobs and economic growth.

   - Explore artisan shops, markets, and local eateries to experience authentic Ghent culture and flavors.

- *Participate in Community Events:*

- Engaging in local festivals, markets, and cultural events allows visitors to connect with residents and learn about Ghent's traditions. These experiences foster cultural exchange and provide insights into the community's values and heritage.

- *Support Local Artisans and Craftspeople:*

- Consider purchasing handmade goods and crafts from local artisans. This not only supports their livelihoods but also promotes the preservation of traditional skills and craftsmanship.

- *Volunteer Opportunities:*

- Many organizations in Ghent welcome visitors to volunteer their time for community projects, environmental clean-ups, or cultural preservation efforts. Participating in volunteer programs can be a rewarding way to give back to the community while learning more about local issues.

- *Respect Local Culture and Traditions:*

- As a visitor, being mindful and respectful of local customs, traditions, and ways of life is crucial. Take the time to learn about the culture and engage positively with residents, fostering mutual respect and understanding.

summary

Ghent's commitment to sustainability and responsible tourism sets a positive example for cities worldwide. By embracing eco-friendly practices and supporting local communities, visitors can enjoy a rich cultural experience while minimizing their environmental impact. Whether you're cycling along the canals, dining at a local restaurant, or exploring the city's vibrant neighborhoods, there are numerous opportunities to contribute to Ghent's sustainability efforts and create lasting, positive memories.

CHAPTER 15: CONCLUSION

As you conclude your journey through Ghent, you are left with a deep appreciation for a city that beautifully intertwines its rich history with modern vibrancy. From its stunning medieval architecture to the lively cultural scene, Ghent offers an array of experiences that captivate every visitor. You have explored its charming neighborhoods, tasted its exquisite culinary delights, and engaged with its warm and welcoming community.

This guide has provided you with essential information to navigate Ghent effectively, from practical tips on getting around and finding accommodation to understanding local customs and festivals. Each chapter highlighted the unique aspects of the city, emphasizing its commitment to sustainability and responsible tourism. By choosing to support local businesses, participate in community events, and respect the environment, you contribute to the preservation of Ghent's character and charm.

As you plan your visit, remember that Ghent is not just a destination; it is a living tapestry of culture, history, and innovation. Embrace the local traditions, savor the delicious food, and immerse yourself in the art and music that fill its streets. Whether you are wandering through its picturesque canals, discovering hidden gems in the bustling markets, or simply enjoying a quiet moment in one of its many parks, Ghent invites you to connect with its spirit.

In essence, your adventure in Ghent is not just about what you see and do, but also about the memories you create and the connections you forge. The city's beauty lies in its ability to inspire, educate, and enrich your life, making it a place you will long remember. As you return home, take with you the stories of Ghent, the friendships made, and the lessons learned. We hope this guide has equipped you with the knowledge and inspiration to explore all that Ghent has to offer, and we encourage you to keep the spirit of discovery alive in your travels.

May your time in Ghent be filled with wonder, joy, and unforgettable experiences.

Printed in Great Britain
by Amazon